LIFT UP HIS BANNER
B E G I N N E R S

t h e   a r t   o f   f l a g   t w i r l i n g

By

Magrate Yap
&
Melissa Yap

Published and Distributed by:
Shachah Ministries International
P.O. Box 763849, Dallas, TX 75376, USA.

e-mail: shachah@shachah.org
www.shachah.org

First Printing. Second Edition. Revised in 2000
Copyright © 2000 by Magrate Yap & Melissa Yap
Library of Congress Catalog Card Number   00-091121
ISBN 1-928799-01-9

All Scriptures in NKJV unless otherwise noted.
Teaching videotapes illustrating the contents of this manual are available.

⚐ ⚐ ⚐ FOREWARD ⚐ ⚐ ⚐

In October 1989, while I was worshipping at Christ For The Nations Institute in Stony Brook, New York, a student came up to me and asked if she could worship the Lord with the flags. I consented, for I know that our Lord is a creative God. I had never seen the flags used in worship before, although I had worked with various banners and streamers myself.

As the worship advanced into high praises, I watched her closely and was overwhelmed by the Spirit of the Lord which was indeed present as the flags were lifted up. I became very excited and praised the Lord for releasing His creativity and freedom once again.

After the worship, I approached the student and told her how excited I was to see the flags used to worship the Lord. I immediately asked her for an on-the-spot lesson because I knew in my spirit that it was something the Lord wanted me to explore. This was the same "gut" feeling I had when the Lord put the excitement in me for the tambourine and dance some years ago.

I bought a pair of flags and tried to practice the few routines I had managed to learn but found it very difficult to remember all of them. At that time, there were no flag instruction manuals available for me to refer to and, as far as I gathered, it was an 'apprenticeship' thing.

That afternoon, I mentioned my interest of the flags to a tambourine student that I was instructing. She said she had learned a form of flags when she was in high school. She started showing me what she remembered and it was the very thing I had seen in New York. As we began to worship the Lord with the various routines, I knew in my Spirit that the Lord desired this form of art incorporated into worship and spiritual warfare.

In July 1990 I was impressed by the Lord to write a flag twirling manual. All of the flag routines were given Biblical names and scripture references similar to the tambourine patterns. Flag twirling, in itself, has no real impact in the spiritual realm. However, with the Biblical names and scriptures that go with the routines, it is the Word of

God going forth to accomplish HIS purposes as the worshiper worships that makes the difference. The skill of flag twirling is another dimension of the creative arts the Lord deeply desires to bring back into the church, both for worship and warfare.

Over the years, I have seen how our Lord has miraculously confirmed all that He has spoken, especially when I see throngs of men, women, and even children taking up the flags to proclaim that JESUS CHRIST IS LORD! When the flags are 'lifted up' there is an air of authority that is established in the spiritual realm which cannot be explained except through the Word of God.

"Let the high praises of God be in their mouth,
and a two-edged sword in their hand,
to execute vengeance on the nations and punishments on the peoples;
to bind their kings with chains, and their nobles with fetters of iron;
to execute on them the written judgement-
this honor have all His saints. Praise the Lord!"
Psalm 149:6-9

I hope that you will enjoy this manual not only to learn how to play the flags, but more importantly, I pray that you will raise a standard as you worship God with them.

There are four levels of flag instruction that will help you increase your skill and each level challenges you to different dimensions of the art of flag twirling. Instructional videos and manuals for all of the levels give photographic illustrations to demonstrate the routines. To facilitate your interest in this area, we carry all of the materials you will need.

May the Lord bless you as you begin to LIFT UP HIS BANNER!

Magrate Yap
Founder and Principal of Shachah Ministries International.

ACKNOWLEDGEMENTS

To the **LORD JESUS CHRIST,**
who by His Spirit has revealed the significance of flag-twirling and lifting up His banner.

Special thanks goes to:

Michael Yap

My dearest husband, what can I say. He believes in me more than I believe in myself. I keep reminding him that this task is impossible for me to accomplish for many reasons, one of which,is that I have never gone to college. I do not have a degree in writing and I do not etc....... You think this would deter him? nah!!! He thinks just because I am a good cook that I am automatically a good author! Perhaps there maybe some truth in this. When you cook, you throw in all the ingredients that are there hoping something will turn out, and I guess writing is the same, you throw in all the ingredients that you have and guess what! God makes up for the rest.

Mae, Melissa, and Maxine

To my precious daughters, Mae and Maxine, thank you for praying like crazy. I love you very much. I would especially like to appreciate my daughter, Melissa, who was a constant source of encouragement and inspiration to me. She knew that it was the Lord who wanted this done and she kept seeing the light at the end of the tunnel whenever I was discouraged. She kept reminding me of the vision that God had given me, and with her loving smile, picked up the "slack" the times I found it too overwhelming to continue. And for working toward the Advance I and II levels of the flag set syllabi and manuals.Thank you darling Melissa. Mommy will never be able to do this without you. I love you.

Anna Weberg

This amazing child is like a "refreshing spring for the dried up pastures" who graciously gave her time to help type and pose for this book and worked with Melissa toward the Advance I and II levels of the flag set syllabi and manuals. She is very dependable and she is willing to learn all that is necessary in order to "fill in the gaps" that Melissa and I left undone. These are not minor things I am referring to. These are learning all the computer skills that would normally take weeks or months for me to learn, Anna does it in one afternoon. Her dedication to God and to us as His servant, has blessed me tremendously.

Jim & Marsha Reason

And of course there is that dependable, always available, forever willing Marsha of a friend. If you find grammatical mistakes on this page, it is simply because I did not want her to edit it. She is very patient and longsuffering when it comes to editing because she allows me to be me, expressing thoughts the way my Asian mind thinks. When she sees a "prophetic rebuke" coming, she mumbles a prayer. She tries to acclimate me to the American language... bless your heart Marsha. Then there's Mac Gyver's twin, Uncle Jim, the photographic inserts are his forte. He and the computer are one. Hummmmmm........

Kenji Saito

for patiently taking all the photographic sequences in this book. Without your insight and stability when everything was falling apart, we would have never finished taking the photographs for the instructional pages. Thanks a lot!

Friends

for their contributions to the choreography in this book…
May the Lord bless you all with more of His endless creativity.

HE IS ABLE to those who make themselves available! Hallelujah!
IT IS EASY WHEN YOU KNOW HOW and may I add, when you know WHO is doing it!
God Bless you and I love you.

TABLE OF CONTENTS

ꔕ ꔕ ꔕ ꔕ **Chapter 1** ꔕ ꔕ ꔕ ꔕ

*"...awesome as an **army with banners**."*

Song of Solomon 6:4

This chapter of the Bible refers to the description of the Bride of Christ. She is compared to the wondrous awe of seeing an ***army with banners***. The banner has always been mentioned throughout the Bible as a symbolic representation of an army. In the days of old, banners were also used to represent the different battalions as they went to war. *"You have given a banner to those who fear you, that it may be displayed because of the truth". (Psalm 60:4) "Through God we will do valiantly, for it is He who shall tread down our enemies." (Psalm 60:12)*

*"He brought me to the banqueting house, And His **banner** over me was love."*

Song of Solomon 2:4

God demonstrated His unconditional love by sending His only son, Jesus Christ, so we can return to Him as His children. We serve a God of love and our response to Him should be that of love. Let us lift up Jesus in our lives and let our lifestyles be the ***banner*** that will always display the love of God.

*"We will rejoice in Your salvation and in the Name of our God we will **set up our banners!** May the Lord fulfill all your petitions."*

Psalm 20:5

Whatever we establish according to the Word of God, He will surely hear. As stated in the above scripture, the banner establishes that which is set above and the Lord will hear and fulfill all our petitions.

*"**Lift up a banner** on the high mountain,*
raise your voice to them; wave your hand,
that they may enter the gates of the nobles."

Isaiah 13:2

This scripture, I believe, is one of the keys for Christians to grasp hold of especially in times of persecution. Many of us react to persecution by "going under cover" or "hiding" our faith in response to self-preservation. Yet, the Lord desires that we stand upon His Name on the high mountain with our voices raised in high praises. For it will be the Lord who takes vengeance upon the enemy when we stand boldly to proclaim the Name of Jesus and to lift high His banner. God calls all people who are sanctified, steadfast, and all those who rejoice in His excellent greatness, to gather around the banner and participate with Him to possess the promised land.

"And Moses built an altar and called its name,
The-Lord-Is-My-Banner;"

Exodus 17:15

Moses built an altar and called it "Jehovah Nissi", after he won the battle with the Amalekites. The banner that Moses lifted up was that of victory over the enemy. We know that when God is on our side, no one can be against us.

*"You have **given a banner** to those who fear You, that it may be displayed because of the truth"*

Psalm 60:4

The banner was a rallying point for the Israelites to establish what they believed in and whenever they gathered around the banner, it proclaimed the truth of God that the pagan world did not understand. The banner was also a landmark for the Israelites, as a reminder of God's sovereignty, that they were instructed never to remove.

*"All inhabitants of the world and dwellers on the earth: when **he lifts up a banner** on the mountains, you see it; and when he blows a trumpet, you hear it."*

Isaiah 18:3

"And I, if I am lifted up from the earth, will draw all peoples to Myself."

John 12:32

Jesus was lifted up as Jehovah Nissi-The Lord my Banner. The cross that held him became the pole. The heavens were shaken by the glory of God when the Son of God was lifted high in all the earth. With Christ in our hearts and the testimony of transformation in our lives, we are lifting up our banners and raising a standard declaring HE IS LORD!! Worship is a lifestyle, not just something we do as a ritual on Sundays. The standard that was established when Jesus was lifted on the cross was not only for salvation but also for healing and deliverance.

O come, let us worship and bow down;
Let us kneel before the Lord our maker
Psalm 95:6

WORSHIP - LIFTING UP HIS BANNER

"God is Spirit, and those who worship Him must worship in <u>spirit</u> and in <u>truth.</u>"

John 4:24

WORSHIP IN SPIRIT

The only way to worship in the spirit is to be born again. This means that your spirit is now in touch with the Spirit of God. This simple prayer of asking Jesus to forgive all your sins and then opening your heart to invite Him to be your Lord and Master is all it takes to be born again. With your new, born again spirit, the next thing you should desire is the power of the Holy Spirit working within you. You receive this by being baptized in the Holy Spirit and acknowledging that power through the evidence of speaking in tongues.

"But you shall receive power when the Holy Spirit has come upon you;
and you shall be witnesses to Me in Jerusalem,
and in all Judea and Samaria, and to the end of the earth."

Acts 1:8

You may wonder why you need these experiences mentioned above to worship God. Is not going to church on Sundays, paying tithes, giving to charity and obeying the ten commandments sufficient? When such questions are asked, the only answer I can offer is that although you are sincere, you are sincerely wrong.

Worship is a relationship. If you want to worship God, then you must do it His way. Not how you have been brought up to worship Him as a ritual. The Scriptural way is what I am referring to. These scriptures mentioned are in the Bible. Do not ignore them just because you have not been brought up to understand them or simply choose to block them out just because you know someone who has had these experiences but is not acting like a Christian should act. Do not blame others for what you are not. Not desiring to know and apply all that God has stipulated in His Word is sheer ignorance, pride and/or "spiritual blindness" on your part. Leave the others to argue about the pros and cons of spiritual doctrines. I encourage you to discover all that God has in store for you as an heir to His kingdom.

Therefore you are no longer a slave but a son, and if a son,
then an heir of God through Christ.

Galatians 4:7

"When the day of Pentecost had fully come,
they were all with one accord in one place.
And suddenly there came a sound from heaven,
as of a rushing mighty wind,
and it filled the whole house where they were sitting.
Then there appeared to them divided tongues, as of fire, and
one sat upon each of them. And they were all filled with the Holy Spirit
and began to speak with other tongues, as the Spirit gave them utterance."

Acts 2: 1-4

WORSHIP IN TRUTH

To worship God in truth involves the physical aspect of the believer's life. This often poses a hindrance to receiving the total freedom of worship by not allowing or not being allowed to release the creativity of God to move through us. We are creatures of habit and we have much difficulty in receiving changes that would pose a threat to our "norm". Sometimes pride gets in the way and with pride coupled with fear, we prefer to dismiss the whole issue of the aspect of worshipping God in the freedom that would release His creativity and spontaneous response to us. Many of the churches do not really experience the power of the Almighty God that they serve because their intellectualism has taken over the place of the power of God, which is the Holy Spirit.

The truth involves a changing of our lifestyle and our responsibility to apply the standards, which the Lord requires of us as worshippers. We have often heard the term, "crucifying the flesh", and this is very true if we desire to draw close to God.

"Flexibility is the key to Spirituality". We so often miss God because of our unwillingness to be flexible. We do not need to protect the Lord. In fact, it is just the opposite, we need His protection. Lifting up the banner is not only for worshippers, but also for every believer who desires a Godly lifestyle to be a BANNER for Jesus.

For example, there is *one* scripture that supports the clapping of hands in worship and *many* scriptures that strongly support dance as an expression of worship. However, we exercise more of the *one* scripture on the clapping of hands and less of - if at all - dance which is supported in *many* scriptures.

Let the body of Christ desire to come to the truth that will set them free from being critical, judgemental, or doubtful of the move of God in the area of the creative arts. After all, we do serve a creative God and He desires His people to worship Him "creatively" in spirit and in truth.

There are a few simple disciplines that will help you to lead a lifestyle of a worshipper and express the freedom of creativity that God ordained. They are: Sanctification, Submission, Sensitivity, and Skill.

1. SANCTIFICATION

A) CHOSEN

But we are bound to give thanks to God always for you, brethren beloved by the Lord, because God from the beginning chose you for salvation through sanctification by the Spirit and belief in the truth, to which He called you by our gospel, for the obtaining of the glory of our Lord Jesus Christ.

2 Thessalonians 2:13-14

B) SET ASIDE

Now therefore, if you will indeed obey My voice and keep My covenant, then you shall be a special treasure to Me above all people; for all the earth is Mine. 'And you shall be to Me a kingdom of priests and a holy nation.' These are the words which you shall speak to the children of Israel.

Exodus 19:5-6

C) APPOINTED

But you are a chosen generation, a royal priesthood, a holy nation, His own special people, that you may proclaim the praises of Him who called you out of darkness into His marvelous light; who once were not a people but are now the people of God, who had not obtained mercy by now have obtained mercy.

1 Peter 2:9-10

D) HOLY

Therefore gird up the loins of your mind, be sober, and rest your hope fully upon the grace that is to be brought to you at the revelation of Jesus Christ; as obedient children, not conforming yourselves to the former lusts as in your ignorance; but as He who called you is holy, you also be holy in all your conduct, because it is written, "Be holy for I am holy."

1 Peter 1:13-16:
(ref: Leviticus 11:44)

2. <u>SUBMISSION</u>

A) <u>TEACHABLE</u>

Give instruction to a wise man, and he will be still wiser; Teach a just man, and he will increase in learning. The fear of the Lord is the beginnning of wisdom, and the knowledge of the Holy One is understanding.

Proverbs 9: 9-10

B) <u>SERVANT</u>

Bondservants, be obedient to those who are your masters according to the flesh, with fear and trembling, in sincerity of heart, as to Christ; not with eyeservice, as men-pleasers, but as bondservants of Christ, doing the will of God from the heart, with goodwill doing service, as to the Lord, and not to men, knowing that whatever good anyone does, he will receive the same from the Lord whether he is a slave or free."

Ephesians 6: 5-9

C) <u>UNITY</u>

I, therefore, the prisoner of the Lord, beseech you to walk worthy of the calling with which you were called, with all lowliness and gentleness, with longsuffering, bearing with one another in love, endeavoring to keep the unity of the Spirit in the bond of peace.

Ephesians 4:1-3

D) <u>OBEDIENCE</u>

Obedience is the highest form of worship.
 For the weapons of our warfare are not carnal but mighty in God for pulling down strongholds, casting down arguments and every high thing that exalts itself against the knowledge of God, bringing every thought into captivity to the obedience of Christ, and being ready to punish all disobedience when your obedience is fulfilled.

2 Corinthians 10: 4-6

E) <u>FAITHFUL</u>

"His lord said to him, 'Well done, good and faithful servant; you have been faithful over a few things, I will make you ruler over many thngs. Enter into the joy of your lord.'

Matthew 25: 23

3. <u>SENSITIVITY</u>

A) <u>DAILY QUIET TIME - DEVELOPING A DISCIPLINED LIFESTYLE</u>

Give ear to my words, O Lord, Consider my meditation. Give heed to the voice of my cry. My King and my God, For to You I will pray. My Voice You shall hear in the morning, O Lord; In the morning I will direct it to You, And I will look up.

Psalm 5: 1-3

B) <u>DAILY READING OF THE WORD OF GOD - DISCOVERING WHO HE IS</u>

For you did not receive the spirit of bondage again to fear, but you received the Spirit of adoption by whom we cry out, "Abba, Father." The Spirit Himself bears witness with our spirit that we are children of God, and if children, then heirs- heirs of God and joint heirs with Chirst, if indeed we suffer with Him that we may also be glorified together.

Romans 8: 15-17

C) <u>INTIMACY WITH GOD - DESIRE TO OBEY HIS VOICE</u>

My sheep hear My voice, and I know them, and they follow Me.

John 10:27

Today if you will hear his voice, do not harden your hearts as in the rebellion,...

Hebrews 3:15

Today if you will hear his voice, do not harden your hearts

Hebrews 4:7

He who has an ear, let him hear what the Spirit says to the churches. To him who overcomes I will give to eat from the tree of life, which is in the midst of the Paradise of God.

Revelation 2:7

He who has an ear, let him hear what the Spirit says to the churches. He who overcomes shall not be hurt by the second death.

Revelation 2:11

He who has an ear, let him hear what the Spirit says to the churches. To him who overcomes I will give some of the hidden manna to eat. And I will give him a white stone and on the stone a new name written which no one know except him who receives it.

Revelation 2:17

He who has an ear, let him hear what the Spirit says to the churches.

Revelation 2:29
Revelation 3:6
Revelation 3:13

If anyone has an ear, let him hear.

Revelation 13:9

D) <u>DAILY PRAYERS - MAKE A LIST OF PEOPLE TO PRAY FOR</u>

<u>1. Immediate Family</u> - Spouse, Children, Parents, Siblings

"Be anxious for nothing, but in everything by prayer and supplication,
with thanksgiving, let your requests be made known to God;"
Philippians 4:6

<u>2. Relatives</u>   - In-laws, Uncles, Aunts, Grandparents, Cousins, etc.

"So they said, "Belive on the Lord Jesus Christ,
and you will be saved, you and your household."
Acts 16:31

<u>3. Extended Family</u>   - Those you are discipling, Brothers and Sisters in Christ, etc.

"...praying always with all prayer and supplication in the spirit, being watchful to
this end with all perserverance and supplication for all the saints-"
Ephesians 6:18

<u>4. Body of Christ</u>   - All the different "bricks' that make the church because
                            Jesus Christ is the Chief Corner Stone.

"...but we will give ourselves continually to prayer and to the ministry of the word."
Acts 6:4

<u>5. For those in need</u> - Physical, Financial, Emotional, etc.

"He shall regard the prayer of the destitute, and shall not despise their prayer."
Psalm 102:17

<u>6. For your City / Town</u>   - Bind the principalities and powers, rulers of
   <u>State / Nation</u>   darkness and wickedness.
                            - Cast away all of the enemy's plan of destruction.
                            - Establish the landmark standards of Holiness,
                              Righteousness, Honesty and Intregrity.
                            - Release the blessings of God.

"But the end of all things is at hand; therefore be serious and watchful in your prayers."
1 Peter 4:7

7. For the Nations of the World

"Let my prayer come before You; incline your ear to my cry."
Psalm 88:2

Afghanistan
Albania
Algeria
Andorra
Angola
Anguilla
Antigua & Barbuda
Argentina
Armenia
Australia
Austria
Azerbaijan
Bahamas
Bahrain
Bangladesh
Barbados
Belarus
Belgium
Belize
Benin
Bhutan
Bissau
Bolivia
Bosnia & Herzegovina
Botswana
Brazil
Brunei
Bulgaria
Burkina Faso
Burundi

Cambodia
Cameroon
Canada
Cape Verde
Central African-Republic
Chad
Chile
China
Columbia
Congo
Comoros
Cook Islands
Costa Rica
Cote D'ivoire
Croatia
Cuba
Cyprus
Cyprus, North
Czech Republic
Denmark
Djibouti
Dominica
Dominican-Republic
Ecuador
Egypt
El Salvador
Equatorial-Guinea
Eritrea
Estonia

Ethiopia
Fiji
Finland
France
Gabon
Gambia
Georgia
Germany
Ghana
Greece
Greenland
Grenada
Guatemala
Guinea
Guyana
Haiti
Honduras
Hungary
Iceland
India
Indonesia
Iran
Iraq
Ireland
Israel
Italy
Jamacia
Japan
Jordan
Kazakhstan
Kenya
Kiribati

Korea, North
Korea, South
Kuwait
Kyrgyzstan
Lebanon
Lesotho
Liberia
Libya
Liechtenstein
Lithuania
Luxembourg
Macedoni
Madagascar
Malawi
Malaysia
Maldives
Mali
Malta
Marshall-Islands
Mauritania
Mauritius
Mexico
Micronesia, federated states of
Moldova
Morocco
Mongolia
Mozambique

Myanmar
Nambia
Nauru
Nepa
Netherlands
New Zealand
Nicaragua
Niger
Nigeria
Niue
Northern-Mariana-Islands
Norway
Oman
Pakistan
Palau
Panama
Papua New-Guinea
Paraguay
Peru
Philippines
Portugal
Poland
Puerto Rico
Qatar
Romania
Russia
Rwanda
San Marino
Sao Tome

& Prinipe
Saudi Arabia
Senegal
Seychelles
Sierra Leone
Singapore
Slovakia
Slovenia
Soloman Islands
Somalia
South Africa
Spain
Sri Lanka
Sudan
Suriname
Swaziland
Sweden
Switzerland
Syria
St. Kitts
St. Lucia & Nevis
St. Vincent & the Grenadines
Taiwan
Tajikistan
Tanzania
Thailand
Togo
Tonga

Trinidad & Tobago
Tunisia
Turkey
Turkmen-istan
Tuvalu
Uganda
Ukraine
United-Arab-Emirates
United-Kingdom
United-States
Uruguay
Uzbekistan
Vanuatu
Vitican-City
Venezuela
Vietnam
Western-Samoa
Yemen
Yugoslav-via
Zaire
Zambia
Zimbabwe

United States

Mexico

Japan

Israel

Switzerland

12

4. SKILL

A) TRAINING

Train up a child in the way he should go, and when he is old he will not depart from it.
Proverbs 22:6

Definition:
1. To direct in growth
2. To form by instruction, to educate, discipline or drill
3. To teach so as to make fit, qualified, or proficient
4. To make prepared for a test or skill
5. To aim or direct one's efforts toward or at an object or goal
6. To submit a person to arduous physical and / or mental exercise to achieve a high standard of efficiency.

B) PRACTICE

Moreover, David and the captains of the army separated for the service some of the sons of Asaph, Heman, and Jeduthun, who should prophesy with harps, stringed instruments, and cymbals. And the number of the skilled men performing their service was:.....(v7) So the number of them, with their brethren who were instructed in the songs of the Lord, all who were skillful, was two hundred and eighty-eight
1 Chronicles 25:1&7

Definition:
1. To actively engage in some course of action or occupation
2. Capable of being put to use or account
3. Designed to supplement theoretical training by experience
4. Performance or execution as opposed to theory
5. Systematic exercise for instruction
6. To put into action
7. To do frequently or habitually

C) EXERCISE

i) exercise lovingkindness...Jeremiah 9:24
ii) exercise dominion...Matthew 20:25
iii) exercise authority...Matthew 20:25
iv) exercise lordship...Mark 10:42
v) exercise myself unto Godliness...1 Timothy 4:7
vi) exercise to discern...Hebrews 5:14

Definition:
1. To drive upon, keep busy
2. The act of bringing into play or realizing in action
3. Regular or repeated use of a faculty or bodily organ
4. Bodily exertion for the sake of developing and maintaining physical fitness
5. Something performed or practiced in order to develop, improve, or display a specific power or skill
6. A maneuver, operation, or drill carried out for training and discipline

D) DISCIPLINE

He also opens their ears to instruction (discipline), and commands that they turn from iniquity.

Job 36:10

He who spares his rod hates his son, but he who loves him disciplines him promptly.

Proverbs 13:24

Definition:
1. Instruction
2. A subject that is taught: a field of study
3. Training that corrects, molds, or perfects the mental faculties or moral character for punishment.
4. Control gained by enforcing obedience or order

꩜ ꩜ ꩜ Chapter 3 ꩜ ꩜ ꩜

WHAT YOU SHOULD KNOW ABOUT FLAGS

CHOOSING YOUR FLAGS:

When choosing flags, make sure the tip of the flag is at shoulder height when the ball is held in the grasp of the hand and with the arm fully extended. If the flags touch the floor when extending arms downwards, you need a shorter pair.

LENGTH:

Avaliable Lengths: 28" - Adult
25" - Adult / Youth
20" - Juvenille

WEIGHT:

The flag shafts are made of steel rods and have a ball on the end. The weight of the rod is necessary because it allows the flag to carry an illusion of "weightless" momentum while it is being twirled. Therefore it requires less effort on the arms to move the flag around.

THE SWIVEL TUBE:

Allows the flags to go around a 360° turn.

THE TIP:

Keeps the swivel tube from coming off the metal shaft.

THE KNOB:

The knob is made of a plastic/rubber round ball, attached to one end of the rod.

HOW TO ATTATCH THE FLAG CLOTH:

Place the velcro (hook) on the flag cloth slightly below the edge of the velcro (receiver) on the swivel tube. If the hook is slightly over, it might get caught and will not allow the flag to move smoothly.

THE FLAG CLOTHS:

Are interchangeable. It would be good to iron your flags before using them.
Remember: how you care for your flags refects on your character.

THE FLAG BAG:

Is excellent and spacious enough to keep your flags secure. It is avaliable in many colors.

SYMBOLIC COLORS:

GOLD: GLORY TO GOD
Glory to God in the highest, And on earth peace, goodwill toward men!

Luke 2:14

RED: BY THE BLOOD
For we do not wrestle against flesh and blood, but against principalities, against powers, against the rulers of the darkness of this age, against spiritual hosts of wickedness in the heavenly places.

Ephesians 6:12

TURQUOISE: OPEN HEAVENS
And He said to him, "Most assuredly, I say to you, hereafter you shall see heaven open, and the angels of God ascending and descending upon the Son of Man."

John 1:51

EMERALD: PROSPEROUS LIFE
He will redeem their life from oppression and violence;
and precious shall be their blood in His sight.

Psalm 72:14

ROYAL BLUE: PRIESTHOOD
But you are a chosen generation, a royal priesthood, a holy nation, His own special people, that you may proclaim the praises of Him who called you out of darkness into His marvelous light.

1 Peter 2:9

PURPLE: SERVANT KING
After that, he poured water into a basin and began to wash the disciples' feet, and to wipe them with the towel with which he was girded.

John 13:5

SILVER: PURIFIED 7X
The words of the Lord are pure words, like silver tried in a furnace of earth, purified seven times.

Psalm 12:6

FUSHIA: HEART OF FLESH
Then I will give them one heart, and I will put a new spirit within them, and take the stony heart out of their flesh, and give them a heart of flesh,...

Ezekiel 11:19

HAND POSITIONS

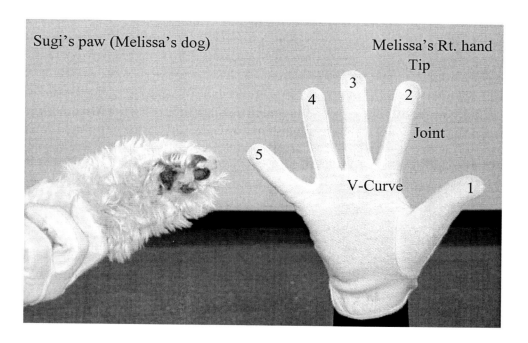

Sugi's paw (Melissa's dog)

Melissa's Rt. hand
Tip
3
4
2
5
Joint
V-Curve
1

Arm Positions

ATTENTION
Arms parallel with body
Flags point up

STATION
Hands on Hips, flags point
outward and upward rest
flags on elbows

GIVE
Arms parallel to each other,
pointed towards the floor in
center

COMFORT
Lift to shoulder height
from GIVE keep flags shoulder
width apart

OPEN
Straight from shoulders
outward next to sides

WAIT
Slightly extended outward to the
side

LIFT
Arms parallel straight up, close
to your ears

PRAISE
Arms lifted to form a "V"
45 degree angle palms face
in.

SURRENDER
As in PRAISE with palms
facing out

18

⚑ ⚑ ⚑   Chapter 5   ⚑ ⚑ ⚑

LET'S WORSHIP GOD WITH THE FLAGS

A) BASIC TECHNIQUES:

1. VICTORY

Scripture: *So when this corruptible has put on incorruption, and this mortal has put on immortality, then shall be brought to pass the saying that is written: Death is swallowed up in victory.*

1Corinthinans 15:54

Definition: To Conquer / The winning of a battle, war, or struggle.

Explanation: History tells us that the christian martyrs in the days of old faced gruesome, horrible deaths. However, the Word of God says that when Jesus rose on the third day, He conquered death. Does this mean that the Word of God is wrong? Could not Jesus' resurrection save us from death? Death to many is the end of their existence and yet many religions try to find life after death. Needless to say, their search is futile because Jesus is the only One who can give them a life after death. *Jesus is the Way, the Truth and the Life. No man comes to the Father except through Him.* (John 14:6)

So what does it mean, "Death is swallowed up in **victory?**" It simply means that our life here on earth is so short compared to eternity. It is awesome to realize that even after the physical death, we do not die! We were not created to die, but to live forever with the One who created us. The question arises, "How do you know that there is life after death?"

The answer is simple. I know what the Word of God says and I have peace. Having His peace and experiencing His love and forgiveness puts me on the winning side in this battle of Life versus death. I have the **victory!** You can have it, too. Start by asking Jesus to forgive all your sins and then invite Him into your heart to be your Lord and Master today!

RIGHT VICTORY

Knob Placement: 2V3
Preparation: Rt. flag in PRAISE
Note: Lt. hand is behind back.

Counts: 1
Rt. Flag: Lower to WAIT
Feet: OPEN

Counts: and
Rt. Flag: Cross to Lt. OPEN
Feet: OPEN

Counts: 2
Rt. Flag: Lift up to PRAISE
Feet: OPEN

LEFT VICTORY

Knob Placement: 2V3
Preparation: Lt. flag is in PRAISE
Note: Rt. hand is behind back

Counts: 1
Lt. Flag: Lower to WAIT
Feet: OPEN

Counts: and
Lt. Flag: Cross to Rt. OPEN
Feet: OPEN

Counts: 2
Lt. Flag: Lift up to PRAISE
Feet: OPEN

VICTORY (Both Flags)

Counts: 1
Rt. Flag: Down to WAIT
Lt. Flag: Down to WAIT
Feet: OPEN

Counts: and
Rt. Flag: Cross to Lt. OPEN
Lt. Flag: Cross to Rt. OPEN
Feet: OPEN

Counts: 2
Rt. Flag: Lift up to PRAISE
Lt. Flag: Lift up to PRAISE
Feet: OPEN

INVERTED VICTORY
(Both Flags)

Knob Placement: 2V3
Preparation: Both flags are in PRAISE

Counts: 1
Rt. Flag: Lower inwardly to Lt. OPEN
Lt. Flag: Lower inwardly to Rt. OPEN
Feet: OPEN

Counts: and
Rt. Flag: Lower down to WAIT
Lt. Flag: Lower down to WAIT
Feet: OPEN

Counts: 2
Rt. Flag: Lift up to PRAISE
Lt. Flag: Lift up to PRAISE
Feet: OPEN

2. WING

Scripture: *"The Lord repay your work, and a full reward be given you by the Lord God of Israel, under whose wings you have come for refuge."*

Ruth 2:12

Definition: Either of the paired organs of flight of a bird, bat, angel etc…
"wings" indicating rapidity and protection.

Explanation: It never ceases to amaze me how a plane takes off from the runway and how the many tons of metal, together with the baggage and body weight, lifts off with such ease and grace. For example, the Boeing 707, at full capacity, weighs 279 tons (575,000 pounds). All this can be attributed to modern technology and using **"wings"** for it's flight. This is God's invention revealed through man because He created **wings** before the foundation of the earth. When man received the revelation to fly, it was through watching a bird in flight.

The purpose of **wings** is not only for flight but also for covering. Take for example a mother hen and her brood of chicks. (Luke 13:34) Whenever there is danger around, the mother hen clucks at her chicks and they all run under her wings for protection until the danger has passed. In the night, the chicks also sleep under her **wings** for warmth and security.

In the Bible, **wing/s** is mentioned over 90 times. Psalm 17:8 says that we are to hide under the shadow of His **wings**. Revelation 9:9 mentions the sound of the **wings** like the sound of chariots with many horses running into battle.

My favorite scripture is Malachi 4:2 - 3

"…But to you who fear My name the Sun of Righteousness shall arise
With healing in His wings; And you shall go out and grow fat like stall-fed calves
You shall trample the wicked, For they shall be ashes under the soles of your feet
On the day that I do this," Says the Lord of Host. (Jehovah Sabaoth)

25

RIGHT WING

Knob Placement: 2V3
Preparation: Bend Rt. elbow in an upward 90° angle, with shoulder slightly pulled back, grip knob with palm facing your head.
Note: Lt. hand is behind back.

Counts: 1
Rt. Flag: Release grasp and allow flag to
           rotate outward
Feet: OPEN
*Note: Keep arm bent & shoulders back.
Do not twist torso.*

Counts: and
Rt. Flag: Grasp knob and twist wrist to
           raise behind head
Feet: OPEN
*Note: Keep flag as close to body as
possible, the flag should be about an inch
from your head*

Counts: 2
Rt. Flag: Continue bringing upward back
           to the starting position
Feet: OPEN

LEFT WING

Knob Placement: 2V3
Preparation: Bend Rt. elbow in an upward 90° angle, with shoulder slightly pulled back, grip knob with palm facing your head.
Note: Rt. hand is behind back.

Counts: 1
Lt. Flag: Release grip and allow flag to rotate outward
Feet: OPEN

Counts: and
Lt. Flag: Grasp knob and twist wrist to raise behind head
Feet: OPEN

Counts: 2
Lt. Flag: Continue bringing upward back to the starting position
Feet: OPEN

WING (Both Flags)

Preparation: Bend elbows in an upward 90° angle, with shoulders slightly pulled back, grip knobs with palms facing your head.

Counts: 1
Flags: Release grasp and allow flags to
      rotate outward
Feet: OPEN

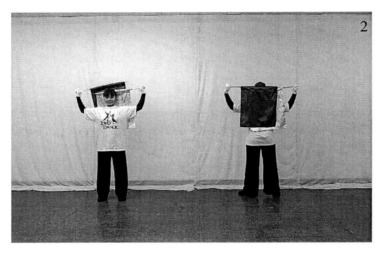

Counts: and
Flags: Grasp knob and twist wrists to raise
      behind head
Feet: OPEN

Counts: 2
Flags: Continue bringing upward back to
      the starting position
Feet: OPEN

INVERTED WING
(Both Flags)

Knob Placement: 2V3
Preparation: Bend elbows in an upward 90° angle, with shoulders slightly pulled back, grip knobs with palms facing your head.

Counts: 1
Flags: Drop flags behind inwardly behind head
Feet: OPEN

Counts: and
Flags: Continue inward motion until flags point down
Feet: OPEN

Counts: 2
Flags: Move back to the starting position
Feet: OPEN

3. ROD

Scripture: *"Yea, though I walk through the valley of the shadow of death, I will fear no evil; For you are with me; Your **rod** and Your staff, they comfort me."*

Psalm 23:4

Definition: A straight, slender stick growing on or cut from a tree or bush. A stick or bundle of twigs used to punish.

Explanation: In the days of the Bible, a **rod** in one's hand was a very common sight. It seemed to be a part of the "dress code" of every person who owned some form of livestock. It is very interesting to note that the word "**rod**" is mentioned over 90 times in the Bible. Many of the scriptures refer to the **rod** as a tool of defense for a shepherd. Whenever there is an animal that threatens the sheep that are grazing in the pasture, the shepherd will either hurl the **rod** at the animal or hold the rod in his hand to fend off the "poacher." This scene lends clarity to the scripture above where it says that the **rod** and staff – they comfort me. It is comforting to know that you have something in your hand that you can fight with.

The **rod** used for the purpose of reproof and correction is mentioned in the bible no less than 10 times.

*"Wisdom is found on the lips of him who has understanding, but a **rod** is for the back of him who is devoid of understanding."*
Proverbs 10:13

*"Do not withhold correction from a child, For if you beat him with a **rod** he will not die. You shall beat him with a **rod**, and deliver his soul from hell."*
Proverbs 23:13 - 14

The **rod** also represents authority. In today's context the **rod** is held by a police officer as a defensive weapon.

*"...and He Himself will rule them with a **rod** of iron."*
Revelation 19:15b

RIGHT ROD

Knob Preparation: 2V3
Preparation: Rt. flag is in WAIT,
           place index finger on
           flag shaft.

Counts: and
Rt. Flag: Use index finger to push flag,
        inwardly, behind back
Feet: OPEN

Counts: 1
Rt. Flag: Continue inward motion until
        flag is parallel with arm
Feet: OPEN
*Note: use thumb & palm only to rotate
flag around. Your other fingers should
remain out of the way.*

Counts: and
Rt. Flag: Allow flag to rotate out to WAIT
Feet: OPEN

LEFT ROD

Knob Preparation: 2V3
Preparation: Lt. flag is in WAIT,
place index finger on
flag shaft.

Counts: and
Lt. Flag: Use index finger to push flag, inwardly, behind back
Feet: OPEN

Counts: 1
Lt. Flag: Continue inward motion until flag is parallel with arm
Note: use thumb & palm only to rotate flag around. Your other fingers should remain out of the way.
Feet: OPEN

Counts: and
Lt. Flag: Allow flag to rotate out to WAIT
Feet: OPEN

ROD Set (for syllabus)

Knob Preparation: 2V3
Preparation: Rt. flag is in PRAISE
Note: The hand that is not in use, is in a fist behind back

Counts: 1 - 12
Flag: Victory, Wing, Rod, Victory (Repeat 2 times)
Feet: OPEN

Counts: 13 - 16
Flag: 1/2 Shield to repeat on opposite side.
Feet: OPEN

RIGHT INVERTED ROD

Knob Preparation: 2V3
Preparation: Rt. flag is in WAIT

Counts: and
Rt. Flag: Rotate flag inward towards
        Lt. side of body
Feet: OPEN

Counts: 1
Rt. Flag: Lower downward
Feet: OPEN

Counts: and
Rt. Flag: Lower out to WAIT
Feet: OPEN

LEFT INVERTED ROD

Knob Preparation: 2V3
Preparation: Lt. flag is in WAIT

Counts: and
Lt. Flag: Rotate flag inward towards Rt. side of body
Feet: OPEN

Counts: 1
Lt. Flag: Lower downward
Feet: OPEN

Counts: and
Lt. Flag: Lower out to WAIT
Feet: OPEN

4. CROWN

Scripture: *"Do not fear any of those things which you are about to suffer. Indeed, the devil is about to throw some of you into prison, that you may be tested, and you will have tribulation ten days. Be faithful until death, and I will give you the **crown** of life."*

Revelation 2:10

Definition: A reward of victory or mark of honor; a royal or imperial headdress or cap of sovereignty.

Explanation: A headdress is part of insignia of an office; be it kings or other dignitaries. The "nezer" (diadem) was worn both by high priests and kings. In the new testament, Paul compares the imperishable **crown** of the Christian's reward to the perishable **crown** of an athelete. (I Cor. 9:25). In 2 Timothy 4: 8 and James 1:12 they mention the **crown** as a reward of life. Having a **crown** on one's head reflects sovereignty, royalty and authority. Even in the world's standards a **crown** or tiara is used by brides, actors, and dancers to denote the same.

The absolute value of all the gold, silver, platinum, diamonds, sapphires, rubies, emeralds and pearls in the royal collection of the Brittish **Crown** Jewels is beyond comprehension. The **crowns** and other artifacts have always been worn and used by the Kings and Queens of England and makes one quick to realize that without question, they stand alone in their priceless ness.

The kingdom that this **crown** rules is made of stones and bricks. Think about the kingdom that we will inherit …streets of gold, gates of pearls. The word(s) **crown/ crowns/crowned** are mentioned over 90 times in the bible.

Revelation 2: 10 speaks about the **crown** of life. It simply means that we as Christians have the privilege to enjoy life here on earth as a victor. This **crown** of life will continue into eternal life.

RIGHT CROWN

Knob Preparation: 2V3
Preparation: Rt. flag is in PRAISE
Note: Lt. hand is behind back

Counts: and
Rt. Flag: Circle flag towards and
above head
Feet: OPEN

Counts: 1
Rt. Flag: Twist wrist to continue
circling flag
Feet: OPEN

Counts: and
Rt. Flag: Extend outward to
PRAISE
Feet: OPEN

LEFT CROWN

Knob Preparation: 2V3
Preparation: Lt. flag is in PRAISE
Note: Rt. hand is behind back

Counts: and
Lt. Flag: Circle flag towards and above head
Feet: OPEN

Counts: 1
Lt. Flag: Twist wrist to continue circling flag
Feet: OPEN

Counts: and
Lt. Flag: Extend outward to PRAISE
Feet: OPEN

CROWN (Both hands)

Counts: and
Flags: Circle flags toward and above head
Feet: OPEN

Counts: 1
Flags: Twist wrist to continuethe flag's circle
Feet: OPEN

Counts: and
Flags: Extend outward to PRAISE
Feet: OPEN

5. WHEEL

Scripture: *And when I looked, there were four **wheels** by the cherubim, one **wheel** by one cherub and another **wheel** by each other cherub; the **wheels** appeared to have the color of a beryl stone. As for their appearance, all four looked alike- as it were, a **wheel** in the middle of a **wheel.***

Ezekiel 10: 9 - 10

Definition: A circular frame of hard material that may be solid, partly solid, or spiked and that is capable of turning on an axle. A circular movement.

Explanation: There are over 45 scriptures on wheel(s).

In James 3:6 the word 'course' is 'trochos'. In Greek, this means 'a **wheel**'. It is used metaphorically with reference to the round of human activity. As a glowing axle would set on fire the whole wooden wheel.

And the tongue is a fire, a world of iniquity.
The tongue is so set among our members
that it defiles the whole body,
*and sets on fire the **course (tanslated as wheel)** of nature;*
and it is set on fire by hell.

James 3:6

In the same manner if we are the axle and we are on fire for Jesus, then we can make a difference and spread the fire for God throughout the nations.

RIGHT WHEEL

Counts: and
Rt. Flag: Lower forward to begin a vertical
circle (clockwise)

Counts: 1
Rt. Flag: Continue circle

Counts: and
Rt. Flag: End circle in GIVE

LEFT WHEEL

Counts: and
Lt. Flag: Lower forward to begin a vertical circle (clockwise)
Feet: OPEN

Counts: 1
Lt. Flag: Continue circle
Feet: OPEN

Counts: and
Lt. Flag: End circle in GIVE
Feet: OPEN

PARALLEL WHEEL
(from up to down)

Preparation: Both flags are at
          ATTENTION
Note: Flags are parallel throughout p

Counts: and
Flags: Lower forward to begin a vertic
       circle (clockwise)
Feet: OPEN

Counts: 1
Flags: Continue circle
Feet: OPEN

Counts: and
Flags: End circle in GIVE
Feet: OPEN

RIGHT INVERTED WHEEL
(from down to up)

Knob Preparation: 2V3
Preparation: Rt. flag is in GIVE
Note: Lt. hand is behind back

Counts: and
Rt. Flag: Lift upward to begin a vertical circle (counter -clockwise)
Feet: OPEN

Counts: 1
Rt. Flag: Continue circle
Feet: OPEN

Counts: and
Rt. Flag: End circle at ATTENTION
Feet: OPEN

LEFT INVERTED WHEEL
(from down to up)

Knob Preparation: 2V3
Preparation: Lt. flag is in GIVE
Note: Rt. hand is behind back

Counts: and
Lt. Flag: Lift upward to begin a vertical circle (counter -clockwise)
Feet: OPEN

Counts: 1
Lt. Flag: Continue circle
Feet: OPEN

Counts: and
Lt. Flag: End circle at ATTENTION
Feet: OPEN

PARALLEL WHEEL
(from down to up)

Knob Preparation: 2V3
Preparation: Both flags are in GIVE
Note: Flags are parallel throughout pattern

Counts: and
Flags: Lift upward to begin a vertical
circle (counter-clockwise)
Feet: OPEN

Counts: 1
Flags: Continue circle
Feet: OPEN

Counts: and
Flags: End circle at ATTENTION
Feet: OPEN

1. SHIELD

Scripture: *"Happy are you, O Israel! Who is like you, a people saved by the Lord, the **shield** of your help and the sword of your majesty! Your enemies shall submit to you, and you shall tread down their high places."*

Deuteronomy 33:29

Definition: A large and oblong piece of defensive armor, protecting every part of the soldier. To protect; to cover; to shelter.

Explanation: Psalm 3:3:

> *"But You, O Lord, are a **shield** for me,*
> *my glory and the One who lifts up my head."*

Psalm 84:11

> *"For the Lord God is a sun and **shield**;*
> *The Lord will give grace and glory;*
> *No good thing will He withhold*
> *From those who walk uprightly."*

When we walk uprightly, we have the assurance that God is our **shield** and we can walk with confidence that indeed He is the lifter of our heads.

Ephesians 6:16 says,

> *"...Above all, taking up the **shield** of faith with which you*
> *will be able to quench all the fiery darts of the wicked one."*

This is a metaphoric representation of a shield that is to affect all of our daily activities. It is important for us as christians to remember to put on the Armor of God every day. The enemy is out to stop anyone who may be going against what he is trying to establish and will attack in any way possible. Be on guard, stay alert, for we need alert soldiers to fight in this battle.

*"After these things the word of the Lord came to Abram in a vison, saying, "Do not be afraid, Abram. I am your **shield**, your exceedingly great reward."*

Genesis 15:1

RIGHT HALF SHIELD

Knob Preparation: 2V3
Preparation: See picture below for starting position.

Preparation: Rt. flag in PRAISE.
Point Lt. index finger in front of you.
Feet: OPEN

Counts: 1
Rt. Flag: Swing to cross on the outside of
the Lt. hand.
Feet: OPEN

Counts: 2
Rt. Flag: Transfer into index finger of the
Lt. hand
Note: flag shaft is in front of the index finger
Feet: OPEN

RIGHT HALF SHIELD
(Continuation)

Counts: 3 - 4
Lt. Flag: Using your wrist, rotate Lt. flag
        in a Victory (with elbow bent);
        End with flag in PRAISE
Feet: OPEN

LEFT HALF SHIELD

Knob Preparation: 2V3
Preparation: Lt. flag in PRAISE.
Point Rt. index finger in front of you.
Feet: OPEN

Counts: 1
Lt. Flag: Swing to cross on the outside of
     the Rt. hand.
Feet: OPEN

Counts: 2
Lt. Flag: Transfer into index finger of the
     Rt. hand
Note: flag shaft is in front of the index finger
Feet: OPEN

Counts: 3 - 4
Rt. Flag: Using your wrist, rotate Rt. flag
     in a Victory (with elbow bent);
     End with flag in PRAISE
Feet: OPEN

RIGHT FULL SHIELD

Knob Preparation: 2V3
Preparation: See picture below for starting
position.

Preparation: Rt. flag in PRAISE.
Point Lt. index finger in front of you.
Feet: OPEN

Counts: 1
Rt. Flag: Swing to cross on the outside of
the Lt. hand.
Feet: OPEN

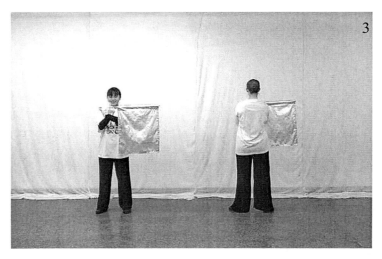

Counts: 2
Rt. Flag: Transfer into index finger of the
Lt. hand
Note: flag shaft is in front of the index fing
Feet: OPEN

RIGHT FULL SHIELD
(Continuation)

Counts: 3
Lt. Flag: Rotate flag to point TIP down,
      Rt. hand grasps the shaft of the flag
      with thumb facing down and palm
      facing out.
Feet: OPEN

Counts: and
Rt. Flag: Release flag into Rt. hand, lift to
      PRAISE.
Feet: OPEN

Counts: 4
Rt. Flag: Complete pattern with one
      Victory.
Feet: OPEN

LEFT FULL SHIELD

Knob Preparation: 2V3
Preparation: Lt. flag in PRAISE.
Point Rt. index finger in front of you.
Feet: OPEN

Counts: 1
Lt. Flag: Swing to cross on the outside of the Rt. hand.
        Lt. (outside) crosses Rt.
Feet: OPEN

Counts: and
Lt. Flag: Transfer into index finger of the Rt. hand
Feet: OPEN

Counts: 2
Lt. Flag: Rotate flag to point TIP down, Lt. hand grasps the shaft of the flag with thumb facing down
        and palm facing out
Feet: OPEN

Counts: and
Lt. Flag: Release flag into Lt. hand, lift to PRAISE
Feet: OPEN

Counts: 3
Lt. Flag: Complete pattern with one VICTORY.
Feet: OPEN

FULL SHIELD SET

(for syllabus)

Knob Preparation: 2V3
Preparation: Rt. flag in PRAISE.
Extend Lt. hand to the side.

Counts: 1 - 12
Flags: Rt. Full Shield 3x
Feet: OPEN

Counts: 13 - 16
Flags: 1/2 Shield into Lt. hand
Feet: OPEN

Counts: 1 - 12
Flags: Lt. Full Shield
Feet: OPEN

Counts: 13 - 16
Flags: 1/2 Shield into Rt. hand
Feet: OPEN

RIGHT BACK SHIELD

Knob Preparation: 2V3
Preparation: Rt. flag in WAIT. Lt. hand is behind your back, and your palm is facing out.

Counts: 1
Rt. Flag: Bring Rt. flag into an upward
         position behind your back (tip
         of flag is pointing up)
         Lt. hand grasp the shaft of the
         flag with the thumb facing up
         and the palm facing out.
Feet: OPEN

Counts: 2
Lt. Flag: Down to WAIT
Feet: OPEN

LEFT BACK SHIELD

Knob Preparation: 2V3
Preparation: Lt. flag in WAIT. Rt. hand is behind your back, and your palm is facing out.

Counts: 1
Lt. Flag: Bring Lt. flag into an upward position behind your back (tip of flag is pointing up)
     Rt. hand grasp the shaft of the flag with the thumb facing up and the palm facing out.
Feet: OPEN

Counts: 2
Rt. Flag: Down to WAIT
Feet: OPEN

BACK SHIELD SET
(for syllabus)

Knob Preparation: 2V3
Preparation: Rt. flag in PRAISE
     Lt. hand in OPEN

Counts: 1-2
Flag: Victory, Wing
Feet: OPEN

Counts: 3 - 4
Flag: Back Shield
Feet: OPEN

Counts: 5 - 6
Flag: Victory, Wing
Feet: OPEN

Counts: 7 - 8
Flag: Victory, Wing
Feet: OPEN

Repeat three times (3x) on alternate sides.

RIGHT SIDE SHIELD

Knob Preparation: 2V3
Preparation: Rt. flag in OPEN with
elbow bent. Lt. index finger
extended at Lt. side

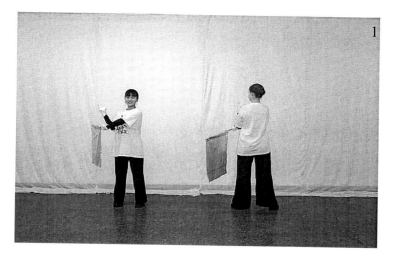

Counts: 1
Rt. Flag: Swing flag downward to cross
on the outside of the Lt hand.
Feet: OPEN

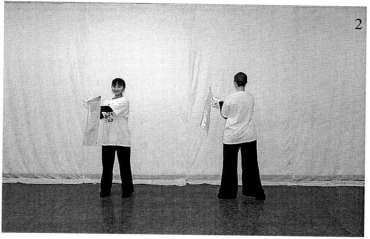

Counts: and
Rt. Flag: Transfer and release flag into
index finger of the Lt. hand
Feet: OPEN

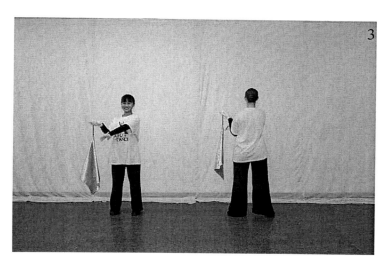

Counts: 2
Lt. Flag: Rotate flag 1x (clockwise)
Note: Like a wheel.
Feet: OPEN

LEFT SIDE SHIELD

Knob Preparation: 2V3
Preparation: Lt. flag in OPEN with elbow bent. Rt. index finger extended at Rt. side

Counts: 1
Lt. Flag: Swing flag downward to cross on the outside of
          the Rt. hand.
Feet: OPEN

Counts: and
Lt. Flag: Transfer and release flag into index finger of the Rt. hand
Feet: OPEN

Counts: 2
Rt. Flag: Rotate flag 1x (clockwise) *Note: Like a wheel.*
Feet: OPEN

54

2. HONOR

Scripture: "Blessing and **honor** and glory and power be to Him who sits on the throne, And to the Lamb, forever and ever!"

Revelation 5:13b

Definition: Reverence, homage, respect and esteem shown to another.
To give preference to, to bow or salute.

Explanation: The above mentioned scripture speaks about the four and twenty elders falling down and worshipping God who lives forever and ever. They honored the One who is worthy of **honor**.

Honor is not an act, but a lifestyle. The Lord gives us an opportunity to practice **honoring** our fathers and mothers in the fifth commandment. (Deut. 5:16) Unfortunately, the generations in these last three decades fall short in exemplifying this character quality. The rebellion in the house sadly results in the dis**honoring** and insolent contempt of God's laws.

When the home starts to practice the fifth commandment once again; to **honor** our father and mother - we will then be able to **honor** God and not be accused of being hypocrites.

*"Now to the King eternal, immortal, invisible, to God who alone is wise, be **honor** and glory forever and ever. Amen."*

I Timothy 1: 17

HONOR

Knob Preparation: 2V3
Preparation: Rt. flag in PRAISE
Note: Lt. hand is behind back throughout the pattern

Counts: 1
Rt. Flag: VICTORY
Feet: OPEN

Counts: 2
Rt. Flag: WING
Feet: OPEN

Counts: 3 - 4
Rt. Flag: CROWN 2x
Feet: OPEN

HONOR

(Continuation - 1)

Counts: 5
Rt. Flag: Lower to OPEN
Feet: Rt. foot to lunge forward

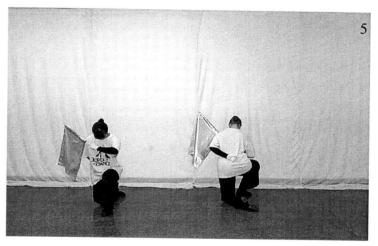

Counts: 6
Rt. Flag: Bring flag to your Lt. shoulder
Note: Bow your head.
Feet: Kneel on Lt. knee.

Counts: 7
Rt. Flag: Out to OPEN
Feet: Transfer weight onto Lt. foot
       returning to forward lunge

HONOR

(Continuation - 2)

Counts: 8
Rt. Flag: Up to PRAISE
Feet: Bring Rt. foot to ATTENTION

3. JIREH

Scripture: *And Abraham called the name of the place, **The-Lord-Will-Provide (Jehovah Jireh)**; as it is said to this day, "In the mount of the Lord it shall be provided."*

Genesis 22:14

Definition: **Jehovah Jireh** – provider: one that provides. To supply what is needed for sustenance or support.

Explanation: Before Abraham took Isaac to Mount Moriah in obedience to God, Abraham must have known that it was not the character of God to require a human sacrifice. Nevertheless, he obeyed God to the last minute before plunging the knife into his son.

God wanted to test Abraham's obedience and Abraham passed the test. God provided the ram whose horns were caught in the thicket to be the sacrifice. Abraham called the place, **Jehovah Jireh** – God will provide.

Today, when we call upon **Jehovah Jireh** – are we really calling upon Him in the situation and predicament that Abraham was in or are we calling on Him only to gratify our greed? There is a difference.

Let's think about it. Abraham could have thought up contingency "plan B" to give God a helping hand by bringing his own lamb. Instead, Abraham trusted God and **Jehovah Jireh** provided!

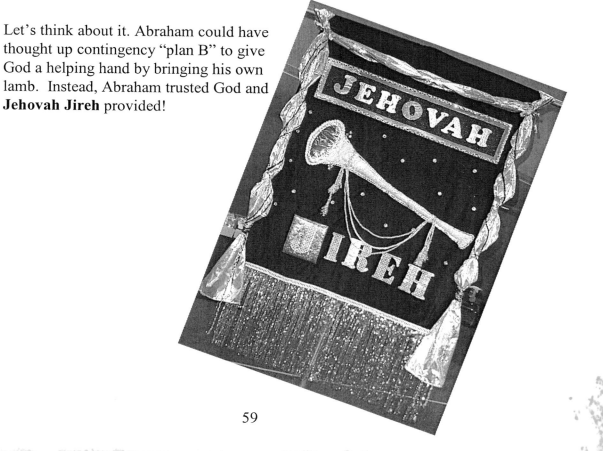

JIREH

Knob Preparation: 2V3
Preparation: Rt. flag in PRAISE
Note: Counts 1 - 4 Lt. hand is behind back

Counts: 1
Rt. Flag: VICTORY
Feet: OPEN

Counts: 2
Rt. Flag: WING
Feet: OPEN

Counts: 3 - 4
Rt. Flag: WHEEL DOWN
Feet: OPEN

JIREH

(Continuation)

Counts: 5
Rt. Flag: Touch Floor
Lt. Flag: Pick up Lt. flag
Feet: Rt. step forward to kneel

Counts: 6
Flags: Lift both flags up to COMFORT
Feet: Transfer weignt onto Rt. foot,
     Lt. foot is extended to the back
     and pointed.

Counts: 7 - 8
Flags: INVERTED VICTORY
Feet: Step with Rt. foot to OPEN

4. MARCH

Scripture: *And he said to the people, "Proceed and **march** around the city, and let him who is armed advance before the ark of the Lord."*

Joshua 6:7

Definition: To move along steadily usually with a rhythmic stride and in-step with others. To move in a direct purposeful manner. To make steady progress. Advancing.

Explanation: Whenever you hear the word "**march**", the following may come to mind: a company of highly trained soldiers of the infantry regiment, immaculately attired in their military uniform, expertly executing the well-drilled maneuvers to clear, concise commands, familiar drumbeats or patriotic tunes.

The whole picture of military expertise is very impressive, but the **march** in itself is a phenomenon. It is a remarkable act, when done in a proper and orderly fashion which starts at a lively pace building up momentum that can be maintained for an indefinite period of time. The key factor is unity. Every step taken to a well-defined measure and in a fixed sequence of time; when every member of the troop is "as one" - bearing a disciplined gait (due to highly-toned limbs), a confident poise, a dignified deportment and a determined, flint-like countenance. The overall effect is a rousing **march**!

In fact, a company of soldiers **marched** in such perfect unison while on a drawbridge, that it gave way and collapsed! This was due to their synchronized **marching** which set up such a high frequency of kinetic-energy oscillations, that the virbrations exceeded the breaking point of the drawbridge framework's energy capacity. An extremely high sound pitch shatters glass in the same way.

In a parallel manner, we, as soldiers of Christ, should **march** to the same beat - the very heartbeat of our Father God, the Lord of Hosts. The rousing jubilation will wreak havoc on the kingdom of darkness, causing a devastating effect.

MARCH

Counts: 1
Rt. Flag: PRAISE
Lt. Flag: Down to WAIT
Feet: OPEN

Counts: 2
Rt. Flag: Down to OPEN
Lt. Flag: Remains in WAIT
Feet: OPEN

Counts: 3
Rt. Flag: Remains in OPEN
Lt.Flag: Forward to COMFORT
Feet: OPEN

MARCH

(Continuation - 1)

Counts: 4
Rt. Flag: Forward to COMFORT
Lt. Flag: Remains in COMFORT
Feet: OPEN

Counts: 5
Rt. Flag: Cross to Lt. OPEN
Lt. Flag: To OPEN
Feet: OPEN

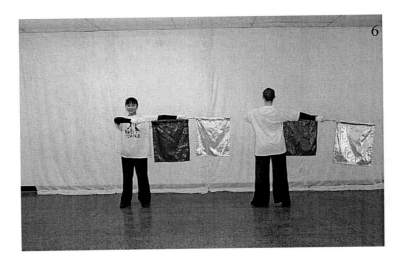

Counts: 6 - 7
Rt. Flag: Rotate counter-clockwise to
       Lt. OPEN
Lt. Flag: Rotate counter-clockwise to
       OPEN
Feet: OPEN

MARCH

(Continuation - 2)

Counts: 8
Rt. Flag: Straight out to OPEN
Lt. Flag: Remain in OPEN
Feet: OPEN

5. NISSI

Scripture: *And Moses built an alter and called its name,* ***The - Lord - Is - My - Banner:*** ***(Jehovah Nissi)***

Exodus 17:15

Definition: A banner is a piece of cloth attached to a staff and used by a monarch, feudal lord or commander for his standard and as a rallying point.

Explanation: When the Israelites were victorious in their battle against the Amalekites, Moses immediately erected an altar and worshiped God. He called it **Jehovah Nissi – The Lord is My Banner**. This battle strategy was unique in that whenever Moses had his hands lifted up, the Israelites prevailed. When his hands were let down, the Amalekites prevailed.

The uplifted hands are a sign of praise to God in the charismatic circle today. As we lift up our hands, we are reminding ourselves that Jesus has already won the battle for us 2,000 years ago when He died and rose again. He defeated death itself!

We will rejoice in your salvation,
*and in the name of our God we will set up our **banners!***
May the Lord fulfill all your petitions.

Psalm 20:5

NISSI

Knob Preparation: 2V3
Preparation: Both flags are in GIVE
Note: Flags are parallel throughout pattern

Flags: Bring flags in a circular motion
      to Lt. WAIT
Feet: OPEN

Counts: 1
Flags: Point down (elbows are lifted & bent)
Feet: OPEN

Flags: Continue circular motion to Rt. WAIT
Feet: OPEN

NISSI

(Continuation - 1)

Flags: Lift up to Lt. side
Feet: OPEN

Counts: and
Flags: Circle to the back of your head
    (counter-clockwise) as in CROWN
        *Note: do not drop the flags behind
        your head as in WING.*
Feet: OPEN

Flags: End circle in Rt. PRAISE
Feet: OPEN

6. CHERUBIM

Scripture: *And the sound of the wings of the **cherubim** was heard even in the outer court, like the voice of Almighty God when He speaks.*

Ezekiel 10:5

Definition: Cherub or Cherubim: A biblical attendant of God or of a holy place often represented as a being with angel's wings.

Explanation: The root word for **Cherubim** is Kevuvim which is plural for **Cherub** or Keruv. Keruv may be related to an Akkadian verb meaning, "to bless, praise, adore."

" *And He rode upon a **Cherub (Cherubim)**, and flew; He flew upon the wings of the wind.*"

Psalm 18: 10

The first reference to **cherubim** in the Bible is in Genesis 3:24. The **cherubim** was used to guard the way to the "Tree of Life".

The Bible mentions **cherub/cherubim/s** at least 90 times. It is interesing to note that 30 out of the 90 times the word **cherubim** is in the book of Ezekiel alone. The prophet Ezekiel was one who "saw" into the spiritual realm. His spiritual insight and "experiences" revealed much of the words by the Holy Spirit in the New Testament.

CHERUBIM

Counts: 1
Flags: Cross downwards
Feet: OPEN

Counts: and
Flags: Bring upward (crossed)
Feet: OPEN

Counts: 2
Rt. Flag: Uncross to WAIT
Feet: OPEN

7. SERAPHIM

Scripture: *Above it stood **seraphim**; each one had six wings: with two he covered his face, with two he covered his feet, and with two he flew.*

Isaiah 6:2

Definition: One of the six-winged angels. A winged angel standing in the presence of God.

Explanation: There are only five scriptures on **seraphim** and they all appear in the book of Isaiah.

Seraphim are described as burning, fiery, gliding angelic beings. The root word is 'seroph' which means to set on fire. So one can conclude that the **seraphim** have fiery colors and move in a flame-like motion.

> *"Praise Him, all His angels;*
> *Praise Him, all His hosts!"*
>
> *Psalms 148: 2*

It is possible that **seraphim** are the praising angels mentioned above, although the specific type of angels is not named.

The ministry of **seraphim** is closely related to the throne and praises of God. (Revelations 4:6 and Psalm 99:1) Cherubim are positioned beside and around the throne and the six-winged **seraphim** are seen as hovering above the throne as they minister in worship.

SERAPHIM

Counts: 1
Rt. Flag: Drop to WAIT
Lt. Flag: PRAISE with elbow bent
Feet: ATTENTION

Counts: and
Rt. Flag: Up to PRAISE with elbow bent
Lt. Flag: Cross over to Rt. WAIT
Feet: ATTENTION

Counts: 2
Rt. Flag: Down to Lt. WAIT
Lt. Flag: Up to Rt. PRAISE with elbow bent
Note: Your arms are crossed.
Feet: ATTENTION

SERAPHIM
(Continuation)

Counts: and
Rt. Flag: Up to PRAISE
Lt. Flag: Cross to WAIT with elbow bent
Feet: ATTENTION

CHERUBIM & SERAPHIM
(SET for Syllabus)

Knob Preparation: 2V3
Preparation: WAIT (see picture below
for feet placement, weight on Lt.,
point Rt. to side)

Counts: 1 - 4
Flags: Cherubim 2x on the Lt. side
*Note: 1st Cherubim is low, 2nd Cherubim is high
repeat for all cherubims.*
Feet: Point Rt. to side

Counts: 5 - 8
Flags: Cherubim 2x on the Rt. side
Feet: Transfer weight to Rt., point Lt.
      to side

Counts: 9-12
Flags: Cherubim 2x in the Center
 Feet: ATTENTION

Counts: 13-16
Flags: Seraphim 2x in the Center
Feet: ATTENTION

<u>C o n g r a t u l a t i o n s !</u>

You have come to the end of the Beginners' level. I pray that you have enjoyed this manual and are encouraged enough to get ready for the INTERMEDIATE level. For all of you who have been waiting so patiently for the completion of this manual and have been praying us through the testings times, I would like to take this opportunity to thank you. Putting together a manual of this magnitude was and exciting experience, but it was also sometimes very overwhelming. Thank you once again for all your support. I pray that God will bless you as you continue to worship Him.